C. S. LEWIS: The Man and his God

RICHARD HARRIES, who is Dean of King's College, London, is shortly to become Bishop of Oxford. He was born in 1936 and educated at Selwyn College, Cambridge, and Cuddesdon Theological College. A priest of the Church of England, he has spent much of his ministry in parish life including six years in Hampstead and nine years as Vicar of Fulham (All Saints). He was on the staff of Wells Theological College and retains an interest in ordination training as Chairman of the Southwark Ordination Course. His main academic interests are the relationship between religion and literature and Christian ethics. He has written widely on the ethics of war, revolution and the nuclear issue.

Mr Harries is the author of numerous books, the most recent being *Christianity and War in a Nuclear Age* (Mowbrays, 1986), *The One Genius: Through the Year with Austin Farrer* (SPCK, 1987), and *Reinhold Niebuhr and the Issues of Our Time* (Mowbrays, 1986). He also wrote *Prayer and the Pursuit of Happiness*, the Archbishop of Canterbury's Lent Book for 1985 (Fount Paperbacks).

Mr Harries is married to a doctor, and they have one son and one daughter.

RICHARD HARRIES

C. S. LEWIS:

The Man and his God

Collins
FOUNT PAPERBACKS

First published in Great Britain in 1987 by Fount Paperbacks, London

Copyright © Richard Harries 1987

Typeset by V & M Graphics Ltd, Aylesbury, Bucks
Made and printed in Great Britain by
William Collins Sons & Co. Ltd, Glasgow

For John and Edna

In 1986 my colleague Dr Brian Horne gave a series of lectures in St Albans on "Charles Williams and His Circle", and he invited me to share in this course by giving the lectures on C. S. Lewis. During the same period I gave six talks on C. S. Lewis on BBC Radio 4. Publication was suggested and so, expanded and rewritten in places, here is the book. I am grateful to Gill Ryeland for typing it.

Richard Harries
King's College, London
August 1986

Contents

CHAPTER ONE

The Continuing Appeal of C.S. Lewis

C.S. Lewis died more than twenty years ago but his books still sell millions of copies, particularly in America, where there are C.S. Lewis sweatshirts, C.S. Lewis calendars and C.S. Lewis bumper stickers. How are we to account for this popularity?

First, people see in Lewis what must, on any historical view, be called mainstream Christianity. He is read equally by Roman Catholics and Evangelicals, Anglicans and Presbyterians, Methodists and Lutherans. Christians of all persuasions see in him the central tenets of historic Christianity. Although Lewis became an Anglican (an Episcopalian, as it is known in some parts of the world), he always tried to avoid propagating a merely denominational view of the faith. His theme, from his earliest writings to the last, was "Mere Christianity". It may seem astounding that an exposition of orthodox Christianity should, for that reason alone, have such appeal, but such has been the variety and confusion of conflicting versions of the faith in recent years that people have come to hunger for what they were brought up to believe even if for many years they disbelieved it.

C.S. Lewis said about a book by Austin Farrer:

We have been deluged with theologies in which the most flamboyant pretensions to novelty and daring co-exist with the greatest thinness and flatness of actual content; Dr Farrer, remaining patient, modest and orthodox, opens new horizons to us on every other page.[1]

What Lewis wrote about Farrer was no less applicable to Lewis himself. He was orthodox; and orthodoxy, when expounded by a person of Lewis's skill, has an attraction with which no sub-Christian theology can compete.

Secondly, Lewis had a powerful mind that worried away at all the old questions and often came up with fresh views on them. An unashamed intellectual, who had read everything and thought everything, he used his intellect and massive learning to penetrate and illuminate the eternal mysteries of God and the world; of man, sin and prayer.

For the early part of his life Lewis was an atheist, but unlike the great Dr Johnson, who said that when young he had talked against religion rather than thought against it, Lewis had thought as well as spoken against it. Although his conversion to Christianity was far from being a merely intellectual matter, his mind was involved at every point, as it was in his Christian discipleship. In this book, for reasons which will be explained, I will be critical of certain aspects of Lewis's thought. So here I would like to pay a tribute to how much I have, over many years, derived from his thinking. On many occasions an idea or an analogy of Lewis has enabled old problems to be seen in a new light. He has imparted understanding, given genuine illumination. He was, and still is, able to do this to so many, not through some influx from on high that bypasses the mind, but because God's grace works through his sheer hard thought.

Thirdly, he wrote so well. Arnold Bennett once gave some advice on writing. He said it was no use sighing, "If only I could write well." You must, he said, "feel more deeply and think more clearly". Lewis's strong, vivid style sprang from that combination. He not only thought with great clarity, he felt with a powerful passion. Englishmen of Lewis's ilk (if he is to be regarded as English rather than Welsh or Irish), or at any rate Oxford dons of his kind, are sometimes thought to be passionless. There is a stereotype of Lewis as the beer-swilling companion, full of jocularity and intellectual talk with his friends in the pub and on walks. This is indeed part of the picture – but only part. There was also great pain and longing. As Austin Farrer said at Lewis's memorial service:

Someone wrote to me that Lewis was a split personality, because the imaginative and the rationalistic held so curious a balance in his mind: and he himself tells us how his imaginative development raced away in boyhood, and was afterwards called to order by logic. Yet I will not call a split personality one brave enough both to think and to feel, nor will I call it integration which is achieved by halving human nature. Certainly reason struggled in him with feeling and sometimes produced bizarre effects: but no one who conversed with him, and listened to the flow of that marvellous speech, could wish to talk of a split between powers so fruitfully and so mutually engaged. No doubt many intellectuals keep a life of feeling somewhere apart, where it will not infect the aseptic purity of their thoughts. If it is a crime to think about all you strongly feel, and feel the realities about which you think, then the crime was certainly his.[2]

The fourth reason for Lewis's continuing popularity is that he wrote with authority; and therein lies a danger. For in an uncertain age people are looking for those who speak or write with confidence. Anxious, bewildered and uncertain themselves, they look to some authoritative voice. Lewis had such a voice. But the problem, dare one say it, is that there has been too much uncritical acceptance of Lewis's thought in Christian circles. That is why it seemed important in this short study not only to explicate the enormous attraction of his ideas but also to look critically at them. Lewis would have asked no less. He was the last person in the world to want an uncritical adulation. But he was a formidable man. Even in his writings he sometimes seems intimidating. People have to summon up all their courage to raise a question against such an authoritative voice. But what Lewis has to give us, still, can only be properly appropriated if we are prepared to argue with him as well as sit at his feet and listen to him.

Interest in Lewis, always high, became intense with the television showing of *Shadowlands*, the film about his life. This extremely well-made film, starring Claire

Bloom and Joss Ackland, won television's top drama awards. It told a remarkable story.[3]

In 1956 Lewis, a confirmed bachelor of fifty-eight, announced in *The Times* that he had married a Mrs Joy Gresham. It was an unlikely match. Joy was an American poet and novelist, an ex-Communist and a Jew who had been converted to Christianity largely through the influence of Lewis's own writings. Four years previously she had come over to Oxford with her two sons. She divorced her alcoholic husband and got to know Lewis. Unfortunately Joy developed cancer. Whilst she was in hospital Lewis went through a civil marriage with her, in order that she could obtain British nationality and live in Britain with her sons. Lewis and Joy did not live together, but when the cancer spread through her body Lewis wanted to take her to his home to die. Despite the opposition of his Bishop, he arranged a church wedding. His bachelor friends were very surprised and some of them horrified; Lewis found an ecstatic mixture of happiness and anguish. For Joy seemed to recover from the cancer; only to relapse again, finally, four years later. This plain, Jewish, middle-aged woman upturned all his ideas of female company. And even Warnie, Lewis's brother, came round to saying that their lives had been "enriched and enlivened by the presence of a witty, broad-minded, well-read, tolerant Christian whom I had rarely heard equalled as a conversationalist and whose company was a never-ending source of enjoyment".

Lewis was an English scholar of enormous distinction, whose influence in the field of literary studies is still with us. He was also a writer of both children's stories and science fiction. This little study deals neither with his literary criticism nor his stories, but is concerned solely with his Christian apologetics. Nor does it deal with either his philosophical arguments or his views on the issues of the day. It is concerned with his understanding of God, with the picture he conveyed of one whose worship is both our duty and our joy.

CHAPTER TWO

The Man and his Joy

According to Lewis's own account, the most haunting experiences of his early life were the touches of an unearthly joy. In his spiritual autobiography he singles out three such moments. The first was the memory of a memory. He stood beside a flowering currant bush on a summer's day, and an earlier memory of when his brother brought his toy garden into the nursery flooded over him.

> It is difficult to find words strong enough for the sensation which came over me; Milton's "enormous bliss" of Eden ... comes somewhere near it. It was a sensation, of course, of desire; but desire for what? Not, certainly, for a biscuit-tin filled with moss, nor even ... for my own past ... and before I knew what I desired, the desire itself was gone.[1]

The second moment came when he read Beatrix Potter's book *Squirrel Nutkin*. He could only describe it as becoming enamoured with the Idea of Autumn, and he went back to the book to re-awake that desire, a desire for something quite different from ordinary pleasure. The third glimpse came from reading a few lines about Balder, the Scandinavian god of light.

Instantly I was uplifted into huge regions of northern sky, I desired with almost sickening intensity something never to be described (except that it is cold, spacious, severe, pale, and remote) and then, as in the other example, found myself at the very same moment already falling out of that desire and wishing I were back in it.[2]

In the story of his early life Lewis describes the outward happenings, his schools, which he intensely disliked, his odd and difficult father, and his time in the army in the First World War. But it was a nameless joy that haunted him. Although brought up in a conventionally religious home he had no obviously religious experiences and whilst young became a determined atheist. But through nature and through his books on Norse mythology, something beckoned him. He loved the countryside, either walking in Ireland, where his home was, or in the Surrey hills in the Leatherhead and Dorking area where he was sent to a private tutor.

I remember ... autumn afternoons in bottoms that lay intensely silent under old and great trees ... or one frosty sunset over the Hog's Back at Guildford. On a Saturday afternoon in winter, when nose and fingers might be pinched enough to give an added relish to the anticipation of tea and fireside, and the whole week-end's reading lay ahead, I suppose I reached as much happiness as is ever to be reached on earth.[3]

The anticipation of books was half the pleasure, particularly those about the Norse gods. For although Lewis did not believe in them they fascinated and enthralled him. Through these myths and through nature he was stabbed by an inconsolable longing. Later in his life, looking back from his new-found religious faith, Lewis came to see these moments as arrows shot from the bow of God. But before that, in the course of coming to belief, he reflected much on the nature of these experiences.

First, he came decisively to reject the cultivation of a particular feeling or state of mind for its own sake. Because the touch of joy was such a wonderful one and because it always faded, he was always tempted to re-awaken the feeling. This was a genuine temptation for Lewis and helps account for the fact that later in life he was so fierce about those like D.H. Lawrence, whom he believed to be cultivating feelings for their own sake. He said that as a child one of the contributing factors to the loss of his childish faith was the attempt to bring about particular religious feelings. Then later, when he found that the thrill induced by reading Norse literature was fading, he found himself making the same mistake. But he came to see that the thrill, the joy or whatever it is, is a by-product:

> Only when your whole attention and desire are fixed on something else – whether a distant mountain, or the past, or the gods . . . does the "thrill" arise. . . . Its very existence presupposes that you desire not it but something other and outer.[4]

This is fairly obvious, though none the less necessary,

because of our tendency to induce states of feeling for their own sake. What is more interesting is his distinction between desire and possession, and his stress on the fact that it is the desire itself that is significant. Lewis recounts how, when the joy which had come riding back to him on huge waves of Wagnerian music had started to elude him and he was lamenting its loss, he remembered a moment when he had tasted the lost joy with unusual fullness, on a particular hill walk on a morning of white mist.

> If only such a moment could return! But what I never realized was that it had returned – that the remembering of that walk was itself a new experience of just the same kind. True, it was desire, not possession. But then what I had felt on the walk had also been desire, and only possession in so far as that kind of desire is itself desirable, is the fullest possession we can know on earth; or rather, because the very nature of Joy makes nonsense of our common distinction between having and wanting. There, to have is to want and to want is to have. Thus, the very moment when I longed to be so stabbed again, was itself again such a stabbing.[5]

Lewis believed that he just managed to avoid the mistake that Wordsworth made all his life. For the sense of loss, of vanished vision, which underlies *The Prelude* was itself vision of the same kind, if only Wordsworth could have believed it. It is the very nature of our life on this earth that we desire rather than possess.

As Lewis came closer to religious belief he made for himself a sharp distinction between enjoying a feeling and contemplating an object. But what was this object that aroused such joy?

> I had tried everything in my own mind and body; as it were, asking myself, "Is it this you want? Is it this?" Last of all I had asked if Joy itself was what I wanted; and, labelling it "aesthetic experience", had pretended I could answer Yes. But that answer too had broken down. Inexorably Joy proclaimed, "You want – I myself am your want of – something other, outside, not you nor any state of you."[6]

In our time, soaked as we are in Freud, it is natural to look first of all for a psychological explanation of such feelings. Lewis, a child of modernity, could not escape the question of psychological origin. In *Surprised by Joy* Lewis stated that he had once enjoyed erotic fantasy and sexual pleasure, but had discovered that what touched him through the Norse sagas was not another form of higher pleasure but something altogether different. When his wife died this conviction was reinforced. In the notebook he wrote after his wife's death, which he kept in order to retain his own sanity, he wrote:

> For those few years H and I feasted on love; every mode of it – solemn and merry, romantic and realistic, sometimes as dramatic as a thunderstorm, sometimes as comfortable and unemphatic as putting on your slippers. No cranny of heart or body remained unsatisfied. If God were a substitute for love we ought to have lost all interest in Him. Who'd bother about substitutes when he was the thing itself? But that isn't what happens. We both knew we wanted something besides

one another – quite a different kind of something, a quite different kind of want.[7]

So Lewis rejected the explanation that his feelings were the result of repressed sexual desires, and came to see them as a genuine longing for God. He hardened up the distinction between enjoying a sensation or feeling and contemplating the object which arouses that feeling. The object, objectivity, became all-important to him and he saw that the feelings he had had were merely the mental track left by the passage "not the wave but the wave's imprint on the sand". All the images and sensations of joy said in the end, "It is not I. I am only a reminder. Look! Look! What do I remind you of?"[8]

Recently Lewis's arguments have been subjected to serious philosophical scrutiny.[9] It has been said, for example, that an unsatisfied desire shows only that you want more of the same, not that you want something altogether different. If you are hungry you want food, and if you become hungry again it is still food that you want. But this analogy with hunger for food fails to convey the sensation to which Lewis was referring. The experience of joy is both satisfying and unsatisfying at the same time. It is not a question, as with food, of being satisfied and then becoming hungry again, but rather the more satisfied you are – as with some intense experience of beauty in nature or music – the more unsatisfied you are at the same time, wanting something more or beyond what has been given. The more intense the experience the more tantalizing it is. This is quite widely documented.

The poet Edward Thomas, for example, in his poem "Glory", about the beauty of the early morning, ends with the line, "I cannot bite the day to its core". Simone Weil makes the same point when, in her discussion of beauty, she says, "We do not desire anything else, we possess it, and yet we still desire something." Interestingly she also uses the analogy of eating when she goes on to write, "The great trouble in human life is that looking and eating are two different operations. Only beyond the sky, in the country inhabited by God, are they one and the same operation".[10]

Another philosophical point made against Lewis is that the presence of a desire for something in no way proves that there is an object. It is not hunger that proves there is food but the discovery of eatable objects. The fact that we are afraid does not prove that there is an object of our fear. This is quite true. But it is a mistake to think of Lewis putting forward a proof for God. In an unpublished manuscript of *Surprised by Joy* Lewis called himself "an empirical theist" who arrived at a belief in God "not by reflection alone but by reflection on a particular recurrent experience". In other words, like St Augustine who ended his quest with the famous words, "Thou hast made us for thyself and our hearts are restless until they rest in thee", Lewis, coming to belief in God by a variety of reflections, could only account for this joy in terms of a longing for God himself.

Another interesting criticism of Lewis of a rather different kind has also been suggested by what is, admittedly, a somewhat odd fact. For after all this talk about joy Lewis, when he came to believe in God, had a very different experience from what one might have imagined. In words that have now become famous he wrote:

> You must picture me alone in that room at Magdalen, night after night, feeling, whenever my mind lifted even for a second from my work, the steady, unrelenting approach of Him whom I so earnestly desired not to meet. That which I greatly feared had at last come upon me. In the Trinity Term of 1929 I gave in, and admitted that God was God, and knelt and prayed: perhaps, that night, the most dejected and reluctant convert in all England.[11]

This is odd. If God is the source to which all our longing for joy points, why such dejection? So, it has been argued, Lewis was working with two totally incompatible views of God and how we know him. On the one hand there is the Greek Platonic view, for whom God is the ultimately desirable object of all our desires. On the other hand there is the biblical view of God the moral legislator, from whom we flee and whom to know requires only repentance. It is argued by some that Lewis's own experience showed that he failed to reconcile what cannot be reconciled. But this is wrong both historically and theologically. It is a matter of historical fact that for most of Christian history millions of people have combined these two approaches to God without feeling them to be incompatible. The classic example of this is St Augustine himself who, like many early Christians, was influenced by Platonic philosophy and who saw God as the source of all that is true and beautiful but who, when it came to the crunch, knew also that God is the source and standard of all goodness before whom we must repent and whom we must obey.

Nor is Augustine's and Lewis's experience theologically inconsistent. For if there is a God, in whose image we have been made and in whom lies our lasting happiness, it would be strange indeed if we had no hungering or longing for a joy beyond all earthly satisfactions. It is what one would expect. Yet, also, if there is a God, then he is one who, by definition, makes a total difference to our life and that difference – of both perspective and behaviour – is not always welcome to us. There is part of us that likes to be self-sufficient, beholden to no one. It may be that, as Lewis found, the stronger the sense that God is the source of an unearthly joy, the stronger the realization that an acknowledgement of this meant some kind of capitulation, a breaking down of a false self-sufficiency.

Lewis believed that what he had experienced was, under different names, the experience of all of us. In one of his finest essays Lewis wrote:

In speaking of this desire for our own far-off country ... I feel a certain shyness. I am almost committing an indecency. I am trying to rip open the inconsolable secret in each one of you – the secret which hurts so much that you take your revenge on it by calling it names like Nostalgia and Romanticism and Adolescence....Our commonest expedient is to call it beauty and behave as if that had settled the matter.... The books or the music in which we thought the beauty was located will betray us if we trust to them; it was not *in* them, it only came *through* them, and what came through them was longing. . . . For they are not the thing itself; they are only the scent of a flower we have not found, the echo of a tune we have not heard, news from a country we have never yet visited.[12]

CHAPTER THREE

The Man and his God

I never met C.S. Lewis but I don't think I would have felt at ease with him; nor am I entirely at ease with his God. Lewis, I am sure, would have applauded this discomfort. He once criticized the low church milieu in which he grew up for being too cosily at ease in Sion, and in particular his grandfather, who used to look forward, as he said, to having "some very interesting conversations with St Paul when he got to heaven". It reminded Lewis of two clerical gentlemen talking at ease in a club. "It never seemed to cross his mind", he commented, "that an encounter with St Paul might be a rather overwhelming experience even for an Evangelical clergyman of good family."

Lewis is right. There is the discomfort we ought to feel, and will feel, before genuine goodness and real holiness. But though Lewis was in many ways a good person, writing hundreds of letters a year to people with religious difficulties, that is not quite the discomfort I have in mind. He was first, a very combative person, which made him such an effective, popular defender of the Christian faith. He leapt at all the weak points in fashionable modern philosophy and hacked them to pieces. He loved an argument, and put his formidable debating powers at the service of the Christian faith, and indeed at the service of everything he believed in: "If you think that way about Keats you needn't come here again", he once roared down the stairs at a departing pupil. With another, who took a different view of Matthew Arnold from himself, he ended up having a fight with two swords that happened to be in the room. This pugnacity must have been exciting, if you could take it. But it does not provide the most lasting defence of the Christian faith. The approach of his friend Charles Williams was quite different: to feel the force of the opposing view, to be sympathetic to its strengths, to concede all that could rightly be conceded. You rarely get the impression that Lewis is sympathetic to the view he is opposing, and often, in his early writings, he simply set up a caricature to knock it down. Lewis was a great battler for Christian truth but sometimes he seemed to forget that the truth he was fighting for was the truth of love, and that the first requirement of love is to try to see with the other person's eyes, however much they might be beclouded by the passing fashions of twentieth-century thought.

The roots of our discomfort with Lewis and with certain aspects of his picture of God go deeper than this, however. I suggested in the first chapter that part of the reason for his continuing popularity is that he was a man of strong feeling; he was also deeply wounded. His mother died when he was a young boy. He was very attached to her, and though he only writes about her death briefly in *Surprised by Joy* it is clear that his whole emotional world collapsed. Then, his father was a very

odd man indeed, with a disconcerting habit of deliber-
ately misinterpreting what his children said to him –
funny sometimes no doubt, but cruel as a settled attitude.
On top of this Lewis suffered a series of sadistic
schoolmasters and bullying schoolmates. He hated
school. Then when he left, he went into the army and
fought through the First World War, being badly
wounded in the process. Many people under the impact
of that emotional battering would have collapsed. Others
would have lain down before life and whined. But Lewis,
as it were, bit the bullet and toughed it out. It wasn't that
he was unsympathetic; on the contrary, he knew the pain
of life right inside, but he made no concessions for
himself and few for others, except when they were in real
trouble. The timid, soft and querulous side of us certainly
finds him intimidating.

And that is not the whole story. One of the strangest
facts about Lewis's life was his self-imposed tyranny by
a woman called Mrs Moore. When one of his friends was
killed in the First World War Lewis offered to look after
the mother. And he did, living with her until she died in
1951, aged nearly eighty. Always a demanding woman,
during the last years of her life she became tyrannical,
even forbidding Lewis to light a fire in his study, in order
to save fuel. For thirty years Lewis chose this way of
living. We will leave the psychologists to root out the
causes of this, but obviously it has much to do with the
early death of his loved mother and his odd, forbidding
father. The salient point is that Lewis had what the
Freudians call a fierce super-ego, an exacting sense of

inner self-demand. He had within him a stern father figure, who both commanded him and made him feel guilty. Unfortunately this rubbed off on his picture of God.

Inevitably we all to some extent create God in our own image. There *is* a true God and he has made himself known. But our personal apprehension of that God never matches the reality. It is always coloured by our own psychology. With most of us this does not matter too much. With Lewis it is a matter of the greatest importance, for he, almost more than anyone else, has been responsible for shaping our understanding of God. He influenced a whole wartime generation in the 1940s with his broadcast talks, and subsequent generations in the 1950s, 1960s and 1970s with his books. His influence today in Christian circles in America is enormous, and even in Britain it is still pervasive.

In H.G. Wells's novel, Mr Polly thought of God as:

> A limitless Being having the nature of a schoolmaster and making infinite rules, known and unknown, rules that were always ruthlessly enforced and with an infinite capacity for punishment, and, most horrible of all to think of, limitless powers of espial.

However distasteful such a picture might be as a caricature of Christian Orthodoxy, it does bring out one important point. The notion of God as stern father or judge or king are only pictures and as such, like all images of God, of strictly limited validity. God *is* in some sense king of the universe, is in some sense the source and standard of our deepest moral insights. The danger comes when we allow one image to have an all-controlling, dominating position. Our images of God need to be continually corrected, balanced and qualified. My worry with Lewis is both about his stern controlling image of God and the way it is so little qualified. In his chapter on the Divine Goodness in *The Problem of Pain* Lewis wrote:

> Those Divine demands which sound to our natural ears most like those of a despot and least like those of a lover, in fact marshall us where we should want to go if we knew what we wanted. He demands our worship, our obedience, our prostration. Do we suppose that they can do Him any good, or fear, like the chorus in Milton, that human irreverence can bring about "His glory's diminution"? A man can no more diminish God's glory by refusing to worship Him than a lunatic can put out the sun by scribbling the word "darkness" on the walls of his cell. But God wills our good, and our good is to love him.[1]

This is a characteristic passage both of Lewis's theology and his vivid, strong style. It is easy to be hustled along and marshalled, to use his word, by the authoritative tone of such writing. But something is wrong with it. It is not the purpose that is at fault. No Christian will doubt that our lasting happiness is to be found in relation to God, or that we fail to see that clearly now. But what about the phrase "He demands our worship, our obedience, our prostration"? Demands? There are certainly situations in life where our obedience can be demanded, when we are soldiers, for example. And Lewis suggests this image when he talks about the divine demands which "marshall" us, in other words, assemble us as though we were on a military manoeuvre. But God is not a Regimental Sergeant Major writ large, nor is the world his parade ground. He demands our prostration, says Lewis. Sovereigns can demand our prostration, and there is a sense in which God is the King of the Universe. But such images are totally inappropriate for deep personal relationships. Moses spoke to God face to face as a man speaks to his friend, says the Old Testament. Jesus is our friend and brother, goes the prayer of St Richard. He is the firstborn in a family of brothers, runs the Epistle to the Hebrews. It is contradictory to think of God demanding our worship, obedience and prostration only until such time as we freely recognize him to be worthy of our worship, obedience and prostration. The two methods are incompatible ways of achieving the desired goal. If you go on nagging someone to obey you, can you really say, when he does finally obey you, that it has been a free choice? We have to decide which of these methods is to be the controlling one, and in the light of both the New Testament and our own moral understanding of what makes for a good relationship, it seems clear that God does not *demand* our worship. He is simply there, like a mountain range permanently on the horizon, to be recognized – like the sky, or the good will of a friend, to be seen by those with eyes to see. He is the source and standard of all that we most cherish, but has left it to us to see with our own eyes in our own time.

Lewis was a moralist. This was the strength of his thought. He sought to relate everything to the holy will of a holy God. But his very strength led him astray in his attempt to understand the role of suffering in creation. Lewis believed that all suffering came to us from the hand of God and had a remedial, disciplinary purpose. When Lewis's wife died of cancer he was absolutely consistent and in a frightening passage wrote:

> The terrible thing is that a perfectly good God is in this matter hardly less formidable than a Cosmic Sadist. The more we believe that God hurts only to heal, the less we can believe that there is any use in begging for tenderness. A cruel man might be bribed. But suppose what you are up against is a surgeon whose intentions are wholly good. The kinder and more conscientious he is, the more inexorably he will go on cutting. But is it credible that such extremities of torture should be necessary for us? Well, take your choice. The tortures occur. If they are unnecessary then there is no God or a bad one. If there is a good God, then these tortures are necessary.... Either way, we're for it.[2]

During his terrible period of grief, about which he wrote so movingly, Lewis felt he was faced with the choice of God the vet or God the vivisector. As he thought and prayed his way through he reaffirmed his faith in the vet, and tried to draw some lessons from what had happened to him. It led him to a new image of God: God the great iconoclast. This iconoclast revealed that his previous faith was just a house of cards and that even his love for his wife was not totally solid.

The tendency to see suffering as issuing from the hand of God is an impulse of only the most devout and heroic Christian mind, such as that of C.S. Lewis. It is none the less mistaken, for reasons which I try to show in Chapter Five. But Lewis was able to go along with this mistaken view because there was, all along, something fearsome, in the wrong sense, about his view of God. Lewis ends *A Grief Observed* by describing the last moments of his wife:

> How wicked it would be, if we could, to call the dead back! She said, not to me but to the chaplain, "I am at peace with God." She smiled, but not at me. *Poi si torno all' eternal fontana.*[3]

Words from Dante, "then she turned to the eternal fountain". Beautiful, moving words. But in the sober light of day what are we to make of a God who gives Lewis, in his late fifties, two years of a blissful happiness that he had been denied earlier, in order to snatch it away, despite all his prayers and entreaties; and that is without considering the question from the point of view of his wife, who died the painful death, and of her two young sons. All this, apparently, in order that Lewis and his wife might come to love God above everything else. This is indeed a jealous God, as the Old Testament puts it. But it is not a god to whom we can give moral assent.

It is a commonplace of Christian thought that there is an unsatisfactoriness about all human pleasures. It was classically expressed by St Augustine in his *Confessions*, and succinctly and beautifully put by George Herbert in his poem "The Pulley". But many human undertakings are in themselves good, and it is only on the basis of a recognition of their goodness that we come to see their radiant source in God himself. Creative work, human care, the conviviality of friendship, art – all these things are worthwhile. Believing they are worthwhile, we move beyond them at our own pace, for it is the only pace we have got, to recognize the giver of such good gifts, who is himself the most wonderful gift of all. But this is very different from the picture of a god who tears everything away from us as soon as we begin to find it full or satisfying, in order that there might be no rival to our ultimate satisfaction in him.

CHAPTER FOUR

C.S. Lewis and the Devil

C.S. Lewis first came to public notice with his broadcast talks in the dark days at the beginning of the Second World War. But it was with the publication of *The Screwtape Letters* in 1942 that he really began to interest and excite the imagination of those who remained at all sympathetic to Christianity. The end of the 1930s dealt a major blow to assumptions that for so long had governed the general ethos. After Munich, T.S. Eliot wrote an essay asking whether Britain now stood for anything more enduring than a collection of banks and a decent rate of interest. Then the war came and many who, horrified by the carnage of the First World War, had been pacifists, reluctantly saw that evil was abroad and that it had to be fought. In a similar way many who had been carried along in the agnosticism of the time began to wonder whether there might not be something ultimate at stake in human life. It was to this new religious seriousness that Lewis spoke. And he spoke about the reality of evil: but in a new way. *The Screwtape Letters* takes the form of a series of letters from Screwtape, a senior devil, to Wormwood, who is just learning the job. Lewis took as his motto some words of Martin Luther, that the best way to drive out the devil is to jeer and flout him, for he cannot bear scorn. Young Wormwood is set the task of leading astray a person who has recently become a Christian believer, but Lewis used this allegorical form to comment more widely on the difficulties and opportunities of Christian faith in war time.

My Dear Wormwood

You say you are "delirious with joy" because the European humans have started another of their wars. ... Of course a war is entertaining. The immediate fear and suffering of the humans is a legitimate and pleasing refreshment for our myriads of toiling workers. But what permanent good does it do us unless we make use of it for bringing souls to Our Father Below? ... We may hope for a good deal of cruelty and unchastity. But, if we are not careful, we shall see thousands turning in this tribulation to the Enemy, while tens of thousands who do not go so far as that will nevertheless have their attention diverted from themselves to values and causes which they believe to be higher than the self. ... How much better for us if *all* humans died in costly nursing homes amid doctors who lie, nurses who lie, friends who lie, as we have trained them, promising life to the dying....One of our best weapons, contented worldliness, is rendered useless. In wartime not even a human can believe that he is going to live forever.[1]

But did C.S. Lewis himself actually believe in the existence of the devil, or was he just using a myth in order to teach moral lessons about Christian discipleship? It was a question he was often asked. In the preface to the 1961 edition of Screwtape (strangely not reprinted in subsequent editions) Lewis denied the existence of a power opposite God and like God. In this view Lewis stood firmly in the Christian tradition, which has never thought of the devil as in any sense the equal of God. Lewis thought the proper question was not whether he believed in the devil but whether he believed in devils, and this he certainly did. He believed that certain angels had abused their free will and become enemies of God, and as a corollary, our enemies as well. They did not differ in nature from angels but their nature was depraved.

There are, nevertheless, questions which many would want to raise against this demonology. First, the existence of devils in no way helps to solve the problem of reconciling a belief in a God of love with the existence of evil in the world. Some, and Lewis was amongst them, have attributed much of the evil in the world to the work of the devil or devils. But this in no way lets God off the hook. If there are fallen angels, God created them in the first place, and he knew they were going to fall. Secondly, there is something fundamentally inchoate and contra-dictory about the idea of a fallen angel. For our free choices are not exercised in a vacuum. Our choices arise out of our personality, our being, which is always situated in a particular environment or set of circumstances. If the angels were created perfect and placed in the perfect environment of the presence of God, how could they have fallen? Then, thirdly, it seems morally intolerable to have hordes of fallen spirits hovering about leading us into sin. There is enough to contend with in human life anyway, arising from our existence as a creature that is at once flesh and spirit, without that as well. So, on philosophical, theological and moral grounds it is necessary to reject the idea not only of one devil but of all devils. There is of course the popular aphorism that the devil's cleverest manoeuvre is inducing us to disbelieve in him. This is only true if we are inclined to under-estimate the forces within us which lure us away from the straight and narrow; and to over-estimate the strength of reason and will-power to control our feelings. In fact, modern psychology has made us highly aware that the rational, conscious part of us is not so completely in charge as previous generations believed. There is much going on in our unconscious leading us to slip, slide and fall just when we think we are most secure. It is true that we can never fully know ourselves and that we often get up to any trick to avoid facing what is in us. But the honest attempt to know ourselves, and the various forces at work within us, seems a more useful and healthy exercise than projecting the cunning of our unconscious onto devils.

So, there is no devil; nor are there any devils. Christian theology does not need them, and the supposition that they exist can obfuscate the real issue of what is going on inside ourselves. Nevertheless, it might be legitimate to employ this mythology in order to explore the nature of sin and evil. How successful is C.S. Lewis from this point of view? It was said of Dante that he put all his enemies into hell. The same principle was at work in the mythological writings of C.S. Lewis. The people he attacks and caricatures are his *bêtes noires*, not least liberal-minded clergymen. In another of his myths, *The*

Great Divorce, a bishop finds himself over the other side, though he does not quite know where he is. He gets into a discussion on the nature of heaven and hell, on whether such words are to be taken literally, and he asserts strongly that all his beliefs have been honestly held:

> "They were not only honest but heroic. I asserted them fearlessly. When the doctrine of the Resurrection ceased to commend itself to the critical faculties which God had given me, I openly rejected it. I preached my famous sermon. I defied the whole chapter. I took every risk."
>
> "What risk? What was at all likely to come of it except what actually came – popularity, sales for your books, invitations, and finally a bishopric?"
>
> "Dick, this is unworthy of you. What are you suggesting?"
>
> "Friend, I am not suggesting at all. You see, I *know* now. Let us be frank. Our opinions were not honestly come by. We simply found ourselves in contact with a certain current of ideas and plunged into it because it seemed modern and successful. . . . When, in our whole lives, did we honestly face, in solitude, the one question on which all turned: whether after all the Supernatural might not in fact occur? When did we put up one moment's real resistance to the loss of our faith? ... We didn't want the other to be true. We were afraid of crude salvationism, afraid of a breach with the spirit of the age, afraid of ridicule, afraid (above all) of real spiritual fears and hopes."[2]

A recent book on C.S. Lewis specifically mentions *The Great Divorce* as being of continuing importance for our own time, and singles out passages like that one as evidence for this. And certainly many people do find that C.S. Lewis still says, almost more clearly than anyone else, what they want to hear. For his books sell over two million copies a year. But, although there are some good passages in both *The Great Divorce* and *The Screwtape Letters* it is perhaps all a little too easy. For if the sincerity and intellectual integrity of liberal theologians can be challenged, so too can that of those who wish to defy the spirit of the age by asserting a firmly supernatural view of the faith. For there is a human motivation for defiantly going against the current as well as for swimming with it. I write, perhaps I ought to say, as one who takes a rather conservative view of Christian doctrine. But the only question that matters is the truth of what is discussed. Pillorying liberal clergymen for their views does not really help, in the long run, to establish the truth of traditional orthodoxy.

The problem with the kind of allegory that Lewis wrote is that it tends to over-simplify. This is fine for children, where it is usually both inevitable and essential, and this is one of the reasons why Lewis's Narnia series is so good. The virtues displayed – courage, truth-telling, loyalty – are such as we can all recognize. The vices lampooned – cowardice, greed, lust – are recorded in every daily newspaper. But in reality life is much more mixed and untidy than that. There is a soul of evil in things good, and a soul of good in things evil. Graham Greene said he would take as an epitaph for all his novels some words from Robert Browning's poem "Bishop Blougram's Apology":

Our interest's on the dangerous edge of things.
The honest thief, the tender murderer,
The superstitious atheist, demi-rep
That loves and saves her soul in new French books –
We watch while these in equilibrium keep
The giddy line midway.

The honest thief, the tender murderer. I don't think
Lewis would have denied the possibility of such people.
But his calling as a combative Christian apologist, and his
chosen weapon of myth and allegory, hardly allowed for
the public recognition of such ambiguities. In his world
black needed to be black and white white.

The ambiguities, ironies and fruitful contradictions of
life are best expressed not in allegory but in novels. It is
perhaps significant that one of Lewis's most perceptive
pieces of writing on the temptations that beset human
beings occurs not in allegory form but in an analysis of a
passage from Tolstoy's *War and Peace*. In a commemora-
tion oration first delivered in 1944 at King's College,
London, and later published as "The Inner Ring", Lewis
explored an aspect of human experience with which we
are all familiar but which is little talked about, the fact
that we belong, or do not belong, to a series of inner
rings.[3] In most of the circles in which we move there is
usually what we think of as a small group or clique of
people by whom we feel subtly excluded. Similarly, there
is as often as not a group of like-minded friends to which
we belong, and to which we feel that "old so-and-so"
does *not* really belong. It is a point that Lewis makes with

great force and insight. It may be that Lewis's extended essays for the general reader will prove more enduring than some of his more popular writing. Nevertheless, he himself was drawn by myth and allegory. He admired Bunyan and wrote an allegory in similar vein called *The Pilgrim's Regress*. He tried to convey in as clear and vivid a way as possible, the eternal verities and the traps that lie all along the road for the unsuspecting traveller. In these works, his imagination, at work in all his writing, was given its head, and as his friend Austin Farrer, who had conducted the funeral of his wife, put it at Lewis's own memorial service:

> It was this feeling intellect, this intellectual imagination which made the strength of his religious writings ... his real power was not proof, it was depiction. There lived in his writings a Christian universe which could be both thought and felt, in which he was at home and in which he made his reader at home. Moral issues were presented with sharp lucidity, and related to the divine will; and once so seen, could never again be seen otherwise.[4]

Sometimes this imagination went over the top; sometimes it was too much at the mercy of his prejudices and too little tempered by his sympathies. It made him oversimplify, and he was often too hard on people and positions with which he disagreed. But he was also unsparing of himself. In his poem "The Apologist's Evening Prayer", a pastiche of John Donne, he wrote:

From all my lame defeats and oh! much more
From all the victories that I seemed to score;
From cleverness shot forth on Thy behalf
At which, while angels weep, the audience laugh;
From all my proofs of Thy divinity,
Thou, who wouldst give no sign, deliver me.

Lord of the narrow gate and the needle's eye
Take from me all my trumpery lest I die.[5]

CHAPTER FIVE

C.S. Lewis and Suffering

When C.S. Lewis was writing a series of "Letters to Malcolm" mainly on the subject of prayer, he heard that his correspondent's son was ill. He quickly wrote back:

> What froth and bubble my last letter must have seemed to you! I had hardly posted it when I got Betty's card with the disquieting news about George . . . making our whole discussion on prayer seem to you, as it now does to me, utterly unreal. The distance between the abstract, "Does God hear petitionary prayers?" and the concrete, "Will He – can He – grant our prayers for George?" is apparently infinite.[1]

Lewis was well aware of this contrast for he had experienced it sharply in his own life. In 1940 he had written *The Problem of Pain*, an attempt, from a theoretical point of view, to understand why an almighty and loving God allows suffering. Then, late in his life after a short but blissfully happy marriage, his wife, Joy Davidman, died and Lewis wrote *A Grief Observed*. This last book, which was first published anonymously, he wrote in the midst of a fierce and bitter grief in order to keep himself going. It is untrue to say, however, that he was unacquainted with suffering when he wrote the earlier book. As was pointed out in the second chapter, his mother had died when he was only eight, shattering his secure childhood world, and he had experienced bullying schoolmates and sadistic schoolmasters. Then had come the First World War in which he had fought throughout, being severely wounded. So there was plenty of personal experience behind *The Problem of Pain*, and there is no discontinuity between his approach there and that in *A Grief Observed*. In both books, however, there is an approach to suffering which is seriously misleading.

Lewis, like all thinkers on the subject, distinguishes between natural evils, such as earthquakes and volcanoes, and moral evils, such as murder and cruelty. In relation to the first, he argues that in order to create free rational beings it was necessary to have a predictable environment. For example, I must be able to predict that fire at a certain distance from me keeps me warm and that too near it burns me. Because fire does not change its characteristics in an unpredictable manner I can adjust my behaviour accordingly. And because the whole of our environment has this regular, fixed, predictable character I can make rational calculations about the future and develop as a free rational being. Some might want to argue the details of this, but it seems to me an inescapable point. Lewis's second point is also the stock in trade of Christian apologetics. Much, perhaps most, of the suffering in the world is caused by the misuse of our free will. But God has chosen to create free beings. Unless we are seriously prepared to be puppets or robots we must therefore be prepared to suffer the consequences of human choices. Some modern philosophers have tried to argue that, on the contrary, God could have created us both free and such that we always freely chose the good. This has always seemed to me nonsense.

So far so good. But then Lewis goes on to develop his theology. God has made us for an eternal good, yet we are born into a world that is fallen. We are shaped by an environment of sin. The dominant character of that sin is that we are swollen with pride. We think we are self-sufficient. We actively resist God, our supreme good. So the supreme function of pain is to break down our stubborn wills. Pain has a disciplinary function. It brings us up against reality, above all against the reality of God. So bad is our fallen state that it needs suffering, sometimes intense suffering, before we are prepared to bow our head or bend our knee.

> My own experience is something like this. I am progressing along the path of life in my ordinary contentedly fallen and godless condition, absorbed in a merry meeting with my friends for the morrow or a bit of work that tickles my vanity today, a holiday or a new book, when suddenly a stab of abdominal pain that threatens serious disease ... sends this whole pack of cards tumbling down. At first I am over-whelmed, and all my little happinesses look like broken toys. Then, slowly and reluctantly, bit by bit, I try to bring myself into the frame of mind that I should be in at all times. I remind myself that all these toys were never intended to possess my heart, that my true good is in another world and my only real treasure is Christ. . . . Thus the terrible necessity of tribulation is only too clear. God has had me for but forty-eight hours and then only by dint of taking

everything else away from me. Let Him but sheathe that sword for a moment and I behave like a puppy when the hated bath is over – I shake myself as dry as I can and race off to reacquire my comfortable dirtiness. . . . And that is why tribulations cannot cease until God either sees us remade or sees that our remaking is now hopeless.[2]

Whilst many Christians will recognize something of this picture it is one that is grossly misleading. First, it hardly seems fair to call the ordinary pursuits of ordinary people "toys". Most moderately decent people are working to earn a living to bring up a family or are looking after children. Nothing very heroic perhaps, but hardly to be written off as "toys". Secondly, the picture Lewis gives is so totally inapplicable to most human suffering. Consider those starving in the Sudan or overwhelmed by mud from a volcano in Colombia, or run over by a car in one of our streets. What kind of God would it be who would inflict such suffering on children or their parents? No one denies that some suffering can be salutary. If I drink too much and have a hangover the next day no doubt this is just as it should be. But suffering is so totally disproportionate and ill-distributed. Too often it is the wicked who prosper in great comfort while pleasant, decent people are afflicted.

I have already suggested that Lewis's great strength as a moralist led him astray. This is also true in his account of suffering. He writes in moral terms about what is in fact inherent in the natural, created order. For example, he speculates that all the bloodshed in nature is the work of fallen angels who sinned before the fall of Adam. They fell and then corrupted the animal world. But this won't work, for even if it were true it would mean that human beings, through their animal nature, would partake of this animal sin, and how then would one account for the alleged innocence of Eden? More important, it is quite clear that much of our capacity for pain and suffering is inherent in created animal life as such. It is not the result of any fall, whether of angels or Adam. Nor is it always related to moral ends. No one doubts that some pain can be used positively. But sometimes suffering crushes people; breaks them either physically or mentally.

Lewis saw pain as the appointed instrument of God for fallen creatures, to break their wills and bring them back to himself. He was consistent in this attitude, even in the anguish after his wife's death. His theology asked him to believe that what had happened to him was directly attributable to God but what had happened was so terrible, could this God any longer be called good?

> No, my real fear is not of materialism. If it were true we could get out. An overdose of sleeping pills would do it. I am more afraid that we are really rats in a trap. Or, worse still, rats in a laboratory. Suppose the truth were "God always vivisects"?[3]

Lewis failed to make a sharp enough distinction between what God merely permits and what he directly allows. Clearly in one sense God is responsible for everything that happens, in that he created the universe. Furthermore, he chose to make a real creation and not simply an extension of his own life, that is, he gave every atom and electron a life of its own. He made the universe make itself, and it made itself by weaving a fabric of life, from elementary particles through cells and multi-cellular structures to us. Where everything has a life of its own clash and conflict are an inevitable part of the whole process. They are inherent in life itself. Clearly there are still major questions – why did God choose to create a universe at all? Is it all worth it? But on this view accident and tragedy are inseparable from any kind of independent life, they are not sent directly from God. And what an intolerable God it would be if they were! We would not think much of a friend who tripped us up on the stairs (thereby breaking our leg) with the stated purpose of seeing how much patience we would develop under adversity. God does not send us evils to test or develop our characters or knock our pride. Nevertheless, when terrible things happen God does not stop wishing us well and working with us. As he wills our health, so, if we fall ill, he seeks to bring what good he can from that illness.

Thus Lewis, reflecting on his own experience, believed that he had come to a deeper faith as a result of suffering, or rather, that the weakness of his previous faith was exposed. God became for him the great iconoclast, breaking down his old ideas. His faith fell down before his personal tragedy like a house of cards. Lewis came to see this as God's work, so that a stronger faith might grow. I have no doubt that Lewis was right to try to draw some such lesson and that God was indeed with him trying to bring some unique good out of a sad situation, some good that only that situation could reveal. But it is very different from saying that the situation had been arranged by God with that purpose in mind. Here we walk a tightrope. Any Christian will want to say that when misfortune strikes we are called to work with God in trying to bring some good out of it. If people are sick, we are to try to heal and support them. If people are starving, we are to feed them and work to prevent such situations occurring again. But this is very different from saying that God arranged that sickness or starvation in order that we might have a chance to show our concern. We live in a world in which accident happens daily, for it is inseparable from a world that is alive with millions and millions of independent lives. Tragedy does occur and tragedy which should be recognized as such, not piously glossed over as something else.

In a perceptive appreciation of Lewis Austin Farrer also exposed his weakness as a Christian apologist, particularly in his account of suffering:

> The moralism which is the strength of his thought runs into excess and overbalances it. When I say moralism I do not mean legalism, an ethic of rules rather than of love. Lewis was a Christian, he was no pharisee. But when he considered man in relation to God he viewed him too narrowly as a moral will, and that relation too narrowly as a moral relation. Man, to Lewis, is an immortal subject; pains are his moral remedies, salutary disciplines, willing sacrifices, playing their part in a drama of interchange between God and him. But this is not all the truth, nor perhaps half of it. Pain is the

sting of death, the foretaste and ultimately the experience of sheer destruction. Pain cannot be related to the will of God as an evil wholly turned into a moral instrument. Pain is the bitter savour of that mortality out of which it is the unimaginable mercy of God to rescue us. When under suffering we see good men go to pieces we do not witness the failure of a moral discipline to take effect; we witness the advance of death where death comes by inches. By failing to keep so elementary a consideration sufficiently in the forefront of his scene, Lewis risks forfeiting the sympathy of a compassionate reader, for all the evidences of a compassionate heart he abundantly displays.[4]

It is the tendency of a devout mind like Lewis's to see affliction springing from the hand of God. The problem with this approach is that words lose their meaning, good becomes evil and evil good. It has been suggested by one recent critic that this is just what happened in the case of Lewis. After fiercely denouncing God as the cosmic sadist, he came in the end to affirm once again his goodness. But in the process did the word "good" lose all meaning?

The dilemma here goes back to Euthyphro who asked in one of Plato's dialogues whether things are good because the gods command them, or whether the gods command them because they are good. Plato took the latter view. It is because we know what good is that we can apply it to God. Lewis took the same view. But could the God that he believed in at the end really be called good?

John Stuart Mill once wrote:

If in ascribing goodness to God I do not mean what I mean by goodness; if I do not mean the goodness of which I have some knowledge, but an incomprehensible attribute, which for all I know may be totally different from that which I love and venerate, what do I mean by calling it goodness? I will call no being good who is not what I mean when I apply that epithet to my fellow creatures; and if such a being can sentence me to hell for not so calling him, then to hell I will go.

Lewis certainly started out with Plato's answer and agreeing with Mill. But did he come, through his terrible affliction, to believe in a God whose standards of goodness were very different from what he had previously acknowledged? For he came to think of God as a cosmic vivisector or cosmic sadist, and only later, after reflection – without denying the bitterness of what had happened to him – did he change this to the cosmic iconoclast who broke him down to build him up. It has been argued that Lewis did so change and though he was himself heroically faithful through it all, his faith was no longer such as to command the assent of rational, moral beings, for the good he attributed to God was no longer recognizable as such. Lewis does, I think, leave himself open to this criticism. It is not his faith that is in doubt but the God he believed in and the kind of justification he gave of that God. There has in fact been some excellent writing this last decade or two on the subject of suffering and the love of God, notably Austin Farrer's *Love Almighty and Ills Unlimited*,[5] a difficult book but one with a touch of genius about it, and also John Hick's *Evil and the God of Love.* Both take a rather different approach to that of Lewis. Because of Lewis's enormous influence it is important to show where he is wrong, particularly on this most crucial of human issues, of how we are to understand suffering. Our starting point is that much that happens in the world is accident and tragedy, and these are contrary to God's will of love for us. He does not ask us to see these afflictions as coming from him. He invites us to co-operate with him in remedying them, so far as we can; and he offers the promise that nothing in life, and not even death itself, can finally frustrate his action in bringing good out of evil. But evil is evil, not a disguised form of good. The Christian justification for using the word good about God is derived from Jesus. First, in that he opposed all the things we regard as evil – physical suffering, mental illness and hypocrisy. Secondly, that though human beings and circumstances conspired to crucify him, yet God raised him from the dead and so he will raise us. It is the will of God to make suffering yield some good. But his particular mercy is to rescue us from mortality itself and to share with us his own immortality.[6]

CHAPTER SIX

Fact, Myth and Poetry

In Evelyn Waugh's novel *Brideshead Revisited*, Charles Ryder queried the beliefs of his friend Sebastian:

> "But my dear Sebastian, you can't seriously *believe* it all."
> "Can't I?"
> "I mean about Christmas and the star and the three kings and the ox and the ass."
> "Oh yes, I believe that. It's a lovely idea."
> "But you can't *believe* things because they're a lovely idea."
> "But I *do*. That's how I believe ."[1]

If Sebastian had been a student of C.S. Lewis one wonders what the reaction would have been to this method of believing. Mixed, one imagines. Certainly C.S. Lewis's observations would have been interesting and illuminating because this was a subject to which Lewis devoted much thought.

Lewis's professional discipline was English literature. He also wrote children's stories, science fiction and some poetry. Moreover, he was personally deeply moved by myths of various kinds as he made clear in *Surprised by Joy*. He was in fact uniquely well qualified by temperament, expertise and experience to reflect on the relationship between Christianity and myth. Towards the end of his life he became somewhat testy about liberal theologians who bandied the word "myth" about so easily and who applied it in a loose way to the Christian faith. Lewis felt, understandably, that they had never really immersed themselves in the myths of Europe, as he had done, and that they had no real feel for the similarities and dissimilarities between Christianity and myth. He was spared the publication of *The Myth of God Incarnate* in 1977. Having produced his own carefully thought out, and extremely balanced view of the relationship between Christianity and myth, it would have tried his patience.

In a paper delivered to the Oxford Socratic Club in 1944 entitled "Is Theology Poetry?" Lewis asked:

> Does Christian Theology owe its attraction to its power of arousing and satisfying our imagination? Are those who believe it mistaking aesthetic enjoyment for intellectual assent, or assenting because they enjoy?[2]

In answer to this question Lewis was certain that intellectual assent and aesthetic enjoyment were quite different. When it came to mythology Christianity was far from being his favourite: "I like Greek mythology much better: Irish better still: Norse best of all." His own experience was, he believed, borne out by European cultural history. For from the twelfth to the seventeenth century Europe took a robust delight in classical mythology. Judged by the pictures and poems of those centuries Europe might have been looked upon as pagan. In fact it was deeply Christian. Lewis came to the conclusion that part of the attraction of myths lies in the fact that we know that they are *not* true. It is disbelief which allows their poetic effect full sway.

Nevertheless, Lewis recognized that Christianity does have imaginative force. First,

> the contemplation of what we take to be real is always, in tolerably sensitive minds, attended with a certain sort of aesthetic satisfaction – a sort which depends on its supposed reality.

Whatever view of the world we take to be true that view gives us a special sort of imaginative enjoyment just because we believe it to be true. But this kind of poetry is the result, not the cause, of belief.

> Theology is, in this sense, poetry to me because I believe it: I do not believe it because it is poetry.

All world views yield poetry to those who believe them by the mere fact of being believed. Even if they are not believed they are likely to have a poetic quality. Lewis said that he himself was always deeply moved by the nineteenth-century myth of evolution; of evolution which struggles to produce human beings who emerge to pit their values against a meaningless universe. He came to disbelieve that myth but it still moved him. For "Man is a poetical animal and touches nothing which he does not adorn."

Secondly, myth is a proper part of Christianity, indeed

an inescapable element in it. The difference between Christianity and some other forms of religion is that in Christianity myth has become fact. This, for Lewis, was the great distinguishing feature. Other religions have had myths of dying and rising gods. But the Christian proclamation is that with Christ this actually happened in the world of historical events. Other religions have had myths of gods becoming incarnate. In Christ God was indeed born at a particular time and place. Lewis came to this belief on 19th September 1931, after a whole night talking to his friends. Later he wrote:

> What Dyson and Tolkein showed me was this: that if I met the idea of sacrifice in a Pagan story I didn't mind it at all: again, that if I met the idea of a god sacrificing himself to himself ... I liked it very much and was mysteriously moved by it: again, that the idea of the dying and reviving god (Balder, Adonis, Bacchus) similarly moved me provided I met it anywhere *except* in the Gospels. ... Now the story of Christ is simply a true myth: a myth working on us in the same way as the others, but with this tremendous difference that *it really happened*.[3]

This factual basis of Christianity was vital for Lewis, and his stress on this separates him from some modern thinkers who regard myth and historical fact as mutually exclusive. But in emphasizing that myth has become fact, Lewis also wanted to affirm that the mythical element or form of expression is still valuable, indeed essential.

Lewis regarded the mythical form as essential in religion because it is only myth that can give us the combined advantages of abstract and concrete thinking. When we think we are, inevitably and properly, involved in abstractions. But when we are moved it is by particular people or situations. How can we both think and feel at the same time? How can the universal and particular be combined? Through myth, said Lewis. For myth allows us to feel and be moved. Yet at the same time it seeks to convey a truth that is universal not particular.

Lewis was willing to draw a conclusion from this line of reasoning which, on this issue, would place him with liberals rather than some conservatives. There is real truth, he alleged, in some pagan myths. The fact that there are resemblances between certain pagan myths and Christian beliefs is not so much the worse for the Christian but so much the better for the pagan. Whilst there is a special illumination in Christianity, there is also a light that lightens every man who comes into the world.

> Those who do not know that this great myth became fact when the Virgin conceived are, indeed, to be pitied. But Christians also need to be reminded ... that what became fact was a myth, that it carries with it into the world of fact all the properties of a myth. God is more than a god, not less; Christ is more than Balder, not less. We must not be ashamed of the mythical radiance resting on our theology. We must not be nervous about "parallels" and "Pagan Christs": they *ought* to be there – it would be a stumbling block if they weren't. We must not, in false spirituality, withhold our imaginative welcome. If God chooses to be mythopoeic – and is not the sky itself a myth? – shall we refuse to be *mythopathic*? For this is the marriage of heaven and earth: Perfect Myth and Perfect Fact: claiming not only

our love and our obedience, but also our wonder and delight,
addressed to the savage, the child, and the poet in each one
of us no less than to the moralist, the scholar, and the
philosopher.[4]

Lewis was willing to go even further than this. Despite all
his insistence on the factual basis of Christianity he
thought that the myth itself (whether or not related to the
fact) could nourish religious life. A man who disbelieved
the Christian story as fact but continually fed on it as
myth would, perhaps, be more spiritually alive than one
who assented and did not think much about it.

There is then no question of C.S. Lewis undervaluing
the place of myth in religion. The only question is, given
his view of its importance, did he still under-estimate its
attractive power in leading us to believe in the first place?
Sebastian in *Brideshead Revisited* stated that it was the
loveliness of an idea that enabled him to believe. Lewis,
in contrast, argued that intellectual assent is primary. The
imaginative or aesthetic satisfaction afforded by the
Christian faith came later, after one had once believed in
its truth on other grounds. Judged simply from an
aesthetic point of view he said he preferred Irish and
Norse myths. Two points can be made in relation to this.

First, as Newman once said, the whole man moves,
logic is but the paper record of it. The whole man that
moves towards religious belief includes the imagination
as well as the will, the aesthetic judgement as well as the
philosophical evaluation.

Secondly, is it not true that, whether true or false, the

Christian story is the loveliest that could be conceived?
The idea of a loving God behind the universe, a god who
came amongst us as one of us, who died for us and rose
again in order that we might share his eternal life, is a
sublime story. In making such a judgement, the aesthetic,
moral and spiritual sides of our nature are all involved. It
may have been true that at some stage in his life Lewis
preferred Norse myths to the Christian story. But in the
end the Christian story captured him and he found in it a
myth which satisfied more than any other. And whilst it
is true that from the twelfth to the seventeenth century
Christian Europe found a vent for its feelings in classical
mythology, nevertheless the story that held the field, that
was central to the life of society as a whole, particularly
the poor, was the Christian one. When St Paul wanted to
urge generosity he wrote:

> For you know the grace of our Lord Jesus Christ, that
> though he was rich, yet for your sake he became poor, so that
> by his poverty you might become rich.[5]

Again, in urging humility he wrote:

> Have this mind among yourselves, which you have in Christ
> Jesus, who, though he was in the form of God, did not count
> equality with God a thing to be grasped, but emptied
> himself, taking the form of a servant, being born in the
> likeness of men. And being found in human form he
> humbled himself and became obedient unto death, even
> death on a cross.[6]

In these and similar statements Paul directs the minds of his readers to God as he has revealed himself in Christ; the picture he gives of God is one that is supremely attractive; attractive not in a superficial prettifying sense but deeply moving, with all the beauty of perfect love. St Augustine addressed God as "Thou beauty most ancient and withal so fresh". God is the source and standard of all beauty. But this beauty is the beauty of perfect love. It is in grasping something of this in the Christian story that we are drawn toward God. The attractiveness of the Christian story, however compelling, is not of course by itself enough. There are hard questions about reality to be asked. Given that this is a sublime picture, does it actually correspond to reality? Does God exist? Did he manifest himself in Christ? Was the tomb empty? These questions cannot be sidestepped. Nevertheless, our answer to them involves our aesthetic, moral and spiritual judgement, as well as a purely intellectual one. God draws us to himself by the magnetism of his perfect love. We feel that drawing power. Certainly Lewis himself did.

CHAPTER SEVEN

C.S. Lewis and Prayer

Someone once said that to believe is to pray and to cease to pray is to cease to believe. It is a sentiment with which C.S. Lewis would have wholly concurred. After he became a Christian believer, prayer was of vital importance to him. Indeed the very words with which he described his conversion indicate this:

> In the Trinity Term of 1929 I gave in, and admitted that God was God, and knelt and prayed.[1]

He prayed on his conversion, and the last book he wrote, just before he died, was a book on prayer. It is, I think, his best work of popular theology. Certainly if I had to select just one of his avowedly Christian books to take with me on a desert island that is the one I would choose. Not only does it contain many interesting insights, it reveals a new capacity to take in and learn from views with which he was not much in sympathy. Lewis, always a combative person, had spent much of his life fiercely exposing the weak points in prevailing fashions of morality and theology. In *Prayer: Letters to Malcolm*, he wrote more in the spirit of F.D. Maurice's dictum that men are more usually right in what they affirm than in what they deny.

Prayer: Letters to Malcolm is a more affirmative and therefore a more mature and balanced work than some of his earlier polemics. It was published in 1965 shortly after Lewis died. In 1962 John Robinson, then Bishop of Woolwich, had published *Honest to God*, whose theme, headlined in the Sunday newspapers, was that our image of God had to go. Instead of thinking of God "up there" or "out there" we were asked to think of him at the heart of things and as the ground of our being.

When Lewis reviewed *Honest to God* he did so with a lordly disdain and academic "put down" that was almost breathtaking. Yet in *Prayer: Letters to Malcolm* he took the general idea of the book on board with great balance and practical helpfulness. Starting from the advice of St Francis de Sales, that we are to begin prayer by putting ourselves in the presence of God, he tried to think through what on earth this might mean or involve. He suggests that first we become aware of our surroundings, the walls about us for example, and reflect on what is really there. Physicists tell us that what seems so solid is in fact something totally unimaginable, only mathematically describable, charged with appalling energies, and that if only we could penetrate far enough into that mystery we should perhaps reach what is surely real. Then, he suggests, we might reflect on ourselves, on the I which is in each of us. Psychologists tell us that the conscious I is only the thinnest film on the surface of a vast deep. Here again if only we could dive deeply enough we might reach that which simply is:

And only now am I ready, in my own fashion, to "place myself in the presence of God". Either mystery, if I could follow it far enough, would lead me to the same point – the point where something, in each case unimaginable, leaps forth from God's naked hand. The Indian, looking at the material world, says "I am that". I say, "That and I grow from one root."[2]

Lewis, even more than most of us, wanted to picture things. He did not like vague, abstract generalizations. As that quotation makes clear, he sought to give the phrase "the presence of God" a meaning related to what he could see, feel and think. This comes out even more strongly in his approach to sensory experiences. When Oscar Wilde was in Reading Jail, and reflecting on life in memorable ways which were eventually published in his long essay *De Profundis*, he wrote, "Religion does not help me. The faith that others give to what is unseen, I give to what one can touch and look at." On the surface there could hardly be a greater contrast between Oscar Wilde and C.S. Lewis. The one an aesthete, a sensualist, a pleasure seeker, the other a stern moralist always on the lookout for ways we might be being led into sin. Yet Lewis was a no less sensual man than Wilde. Indeed, it was one of his abiding temptations to cultivate sensations for their own sake. He felt deeply, he imagined vividly, he loved the physical world about him. Lewis too wanted to touch and look. The difference was that Lewis was able to turn his sensory experience into prayer. Instead of either indulging or rejecting the pleasure of the senses, he came in his maturity to make every pleasure a channel of adoration. In the same way as we do not simply hear a sound but we hear a bird or a train, giving an immediate interpretation to what we hear, so, he said, we could come to "read" our pleasures as the touch of God upon us. It was not a question of experiencing some pleasure and then saying thank you, but rather to experience the pleasure in a particular way was itself to adore. It becomes possible to "read" as well as to have a pleasure so that:

> to receive it and to recognize its divine source are a single experience. This heavenly fruit is instantly redolent of the orchard where it grew. This sweet air whispers of the country whence it blows. It is a message. We know we are being touched by a finger of that right hand at which there are pleasures for evermore....
>
> If I could always be what I aim at being, no pleasure would be too ordinary or too usual for such reception; from the first taste of the air when I look out of the window – one's whole cheek becomes a sort of palate down to one's soft slippers at bedtime.[3]

Once again one notices the way Lewis has integrated into his Christian experience an emphasis that earlier he would have been inclined to reject. For the 1960s was the time of *Lady Chatterley's Lover* and of great interest in D.H. Lawrence generally; not an author to whom Lewis easily responded. Yet, in the mellowing that came in his last years he achieved a fine, affirmative, Christian balance in his attitude to the senses.

Prayer: Letters to Malcolm contains many helpful practical suggestions about prayer. One is his concept of "festooning". He writes that with lines as familiar as the Lord's Prayer we all in our own way "festoon" each petition. That is, we hang it about with our own personal meaning that has been built up over the years. This does not take away from the main sense of the phrase, but gives additional meaning and makes it easier for us to pray. He shares some of his own festooning with his imaginary correspondent, Malcolm. Yet the book is, more than anything else, concerned with the problems posed by petitionary prayer. Some Christians take the view that the most important forms of prayer are meditation and contemplation, just quietly putting oneself in the presence of God and longing for him. Lewis, whilst in no way undervaluing such prayer, was always inclined to stress the crucial significance of petition in Christian prayer. He looked at the New Testament and to him it seemed that when it dealt with prayer it was above all petitionary prayer that was considered; yet petitionary prayer poses such problems. Are we really to think of God acting in the world in response to our requests? If he can so act why does he not do so anyway instead of waiting to be asked? Why, when we do ask, does he not seem to hear? – or at least, why does it so often seem that very little of what we want comes about?

I suppose that for most people, if they think about petitionary prayer at all, the major problem is why such prayers are so infrequently answered in the way that we want. Yet it is characteristic of Lewis that his major worry was something else altogether, something which arose through taking the New Testament seriously, which he did. He first raised the question publicly in a talk to clergyment in 1953 called "Petitionary Prayer: A Problem without an Answer".[4] The problem is that in the New Testament you appear to have two totally contradictory patterns of prayer. There is what he called Pattern A, epitomized by the prayer of Christ in the Garden of Gethsemane: "Father take this cup away from me, nevertheless not my will but thine be done". Then there is Pattern B, which suggests that if only we pray with enough faith we will receive what we ask for: "And whatever you ask in prayer, you will receive, if you have faith" (Matthew 21:22). Lewis confessed himself baffled and ended, "I come to you, reverend Fathers, for guidance. How am I to pray this very night?" Thirty years later in *Prayer: Letters to Malcolm* the problem was still very much on his mind. All he could think was that the prayer of faith, of praying expecting to receive, referred to a degree of faith which most believers never experienced. It was the prayer of God's fellow-worker who was so united with God at certain moments that something of the divine fore-knowledge entered his mind.[5]

But why should we ask God for things? And why should the New Testament lay such stress on prayers of petition? For if God is God he knows what we want before we ask, and if he is good he is doing all he can anyway. Lewis's answer was that God had delegated all he possibly could to us and that he had chosen to work his purpose in the world through us, his agents. Lewis was fond of a dictum of Pascal, "God instituted prayer in order to lend to his creatures the dignity of causality". In other words, God has such respect for us that he allows our prayers to be a real factor in shaping the destiny of the world. And Lewis did really think that prayer made a difference. Whilst agreeing that no one can ever prove that something comes about as a result of prayer, he gives a personal example of someone very sick recovering and another of when he felt himself being summoned by the Holy Spirit to go and visit his barber, who had been praying ardently that Lewis would call because he was in trouble and needed to talk to him. Yet, for Lewis, there was something more important than what was prayed for coming about. What mattered, he said, was "being heard", having our requests taken into account. We can bear to be refused but not to be ignored. But how can we tell whether our request really has been taken into account and refused, or just uttered in a void because there is no God to take it into account? Lewis himself had to face this dilemma in a most painful way, for when his wife died it was the thought of all the petitions they had offered that seared through him. He wrote in his diary:

What chokes every prayer and every hope is the memory of all the prayers H and I offered and all the false hopes we had. Not hopes raised merely by our own wishful thinking; hopes encouraged, even forced upon us, by false diagnoses, by X-ray photographs, by strange remissions, by one temporary recovery that might have ranked as a miracle. Step by step we were "led up the garden path". Time after time, when

He seemed most gracious He was really preparing the next
torture.[6]

As he worked his way through his grief Lewis came to
understand what had happened to him as a shattering
insight into his own weak faith. He came to call God the
great iconoclast, who had shown up his faith as no more
substantial than a house of cards. This view of God, as I
have already suggested, has great difficulties. Yet it may
have been at this time that Lewis thought his way
through to an even more unsettling picture of God.

Some years earlier, in 1959, he had written an article
for an American magazine entitled "The Efficacy of
Prayer".[7] In it he drew attention to the fact that Christ, in
the Garden of Gethsemane, had had his prayer that the
cup of suffering might be taken from him, refused. Lewis
floated the thought that for newcomers to belief or for
those who are weak in faith, God really does answer our
prayers in the way we most want. But perhaps God
forsakes those who serve him best, for it is Jesus himself
who is least comforted by God at the hour of his greatest
need. Lewis concluded that there was a mystery here that
he had neither the power nor the courage to explore. Yet,
before he died in 1963, he did explore it. In *Prayer:
Letters to Malcolm* he meditated on the last week of
Christ's life, observing there the human situation writ
large: every door slammed shut as you reach it, every rope
breaking when you seize it. It made him wonder whether
we had even begun to understand what is involved in the
very concept of creation.

If God will create, He will make something to be, and yet to be not Himself. To be created is, in some sense, to be ejected or separated. Can it be that the more perfect the creature is, the further this separation must at some point be pushed? It is saints, not common people, who experience the "dark night". It is men and angels, not beasts, who rebel. Inanimate matter sleeps in the bosom of the father. The "hiddenness" of God perhaps presses most painfully on those who are in another way nearest to Him, and therefore God Himself, made man, will of all men be by God most forsaken?[8]

It was a passage that clearly reflected his own experience in the anguish of Joy's illness.

CHAPTER EIGHT

Love

There are few experiences more predictable or less helpful than the average Christian sermon on love. Before the preacher has gone two sentences he has identified Christian love with unselfishness or said that liking and loving are not the same. Lewis said that he set out to write a book about love on the same easy assumptions, but he soon realized that the whole subject is much more teasing and, we might add, much more interesting, than that. For understanding the true nature of love is not easy. It is not at all obvious how we should relate the divine love to human love, or how our various kinds of human love should be related to one another. Indeed Lewis ends the book he wrote on the subject, *The Four Loves*, on a note of humility, offering only suggestions and open to the possibility of any reader having much better ideas.

Lewis deals with four forms of love: affection, friendship, eros and charity. The strength of his approach lies in his twin stress. First, he insists that all our human loves are, quite rightly, rooted in earthly instinct. Affection, friendship and erotic love arise out of our physical, instinctual nature. There is no false spirituality, no disparaging ordinary human experiences and pleasures.

As is well known, Lewis had a close circle of male friends with whom he met regularly to talk, walk and drink beer – amongst them Tolkien and Charles Williams. For the long years of his bachelorhood, this circle was second only to God as the centre of his life. It was as a Christian as well as a human being that he valued such down-to-earth human friendship: he appreciated it as an aspect of the good world in which a good God has placed us. Secondly, however, he argued that all our human loves have to be set under and ordered by the divine love; and that if this does not happen they can go badly wrong, can indeed become demonic. It is obvious that this can happen when a person acts on the dictum "All for love", but Lewis was adamant that family affection and deep friendship could become equally poisonous unless they were ordered aright in subservience to the divine love. Friendship, for example, however altruistic, was neither more nor less divine than erotic love. Both need to be permeated by the love that is from above.

> Friendship, then, like the other natural loves, is unable to save itself. In reality, because it is spiritual and therefore faces a subtler enemy, it must, even more wholeheartedly than they, invoke the divine protection if it hopes to remain sweet. For consider how narrow its true path is. It must not become what the people call a "mutual admiration society"; yet if it is not full of mutual admiration, of Appreciative love, it is not Friendship at all.

Pride can creep into even a religious friendship:

For then it will seem to us that we – we four or five – have chosen one another, the insight of each finding the intrinsic beauty of the rest, like to like, a voluntary nobility; that we have ascended above the rest of mankind by our native powers. The other loves do not invite the same illusion. Affection obviously requires kinship or at least proximities which never depended on our own choice. And as for Eros, half the love songs and half the love poems in the world will tell you that the Beloved is your fate or destiny, no more your choice than a thunderbolt.

But in reality our friendships are neither chance nor chosen by us alone:

A secret Master of the Ceremonies has been at work. Christ, who said to the disciples, "Ye have not chosen me, but I have chosen you", can truly say to every group of Christian friends, "You have not chosen one another but I have chosen you for one another". The Friendship is not a reward for our discrimination and good taste in finding one another out. It is the instrument by which God reveals to each the beauties of all the others. They are no greater than the beauties of a thousand other men; by Friendship God opens our eyes to them. They are, like all beauties, derived from Him, and then, in a good Friendship, increased by Him through the Friendship itself, so that it is His instrument for creating as well as for revealing. At this feast it is He who has spread the board and it is He who has chosen the guests. It is He, we may dare to hope, who sometimes does, and always should, preside. Let us not reckon without our Host.[1]

So *The Four Loves* has two themes running through it. One is the affirmation of affection and friendship and erotic love. The other is the snares and pitfalls that these loves can fall into, the illusion that can take hold of them, if they fail to observe that divine love is a jealous love that needs to be put before all other loves.

Lewis begins his book by drawing a contrast between gift love and need love. Both, he says, are genuine forms of love. He refuses to deny the word love to our need for others. The child who comes to his mother for comfort, or a friend who goes to a friend for good advice, are both expressing a perfectly proper form of love. Giving is not the only form of love. Sometimes it is better to receive than to give, for refusing to receive can be a form of pride. Above all, in our relationship with God we are receivers and the prime form of love is an expression of our need for him. So human beings have three main forms of love, which we can show both to our fellow creatures and to God. Need love, giving love and appreciative love – the love which appreciates, admires and in the case of God, worships; the love which exults in the other for his or her own sake.

> Need-love cries to God from our poverty; Gift-love longs to serve, or even to suffer for, God; Appreciative love says: "We give thanks to thee for thy great glory." Need-love says of a woman "I cannot live without her"; Gift-love longs to give her happiness, comfort, protection – if possible, wealth; Appreciative love gazes and holds its breath and is silent, rejoices that such a wonder should exist even if not for him, will not be wholly dejected by losing her, would rather have it so than never to have seen her at all.[2]

None of these three forms of love can stand on their own without grace, or if they try to, they become perverted. It is quite possible, for example, for us to take a secret pride in our sense of need before God, just as it is to take a secret pride in what we might do for God. We therefore need grace through and through, in all we are and do, that our sense of need before God may be without any self-regard and our giving without narcissism.

What though of God's love? There is no need in God himself, says Lewis.

> God is love. Again, "Herein is love, not that we loved God but that He loved us" (1 John 4:10). We must not begin with mysticism, with the creature's love for God, or with the wonderful foretastes of the fruition of God vouchsafed to some in their earthly life. We begin at the real beginning, with love as the Divine energy. This primal love is Gift-love. In God there is no hunger that needs to be filled, only plenteousness that desires to give.[3]

Of course in one sense that is right. In the life of the Blessed Trinity there is perfect fulfilment of mutual giving and receiving. The life of the Godhead is complete in itself. God did not, as I once heard an American Evangelist claim, create the world because he was lonely. He had no unmet needs. There is no gaping void in God which he sought to fill by creating a world. Yet, that having been said, God in his love for us has made himself vulnerable to us; has in a sense put himself in a position of need before us. An analogy can be drawn with a family who, having children of their own, decide to adopt another child. They have no need. With three children of their own they are complete as a family unit. But they decide to adopt, and once they do they find themselves vulnerable to their new child. They can be hurt and delighted by her. They gain much extra happiness and sometimes suffer heartbreak. They give to the child, but they also have a need-love for their adopted child: not a hole to be filled, but a heart that can be delighted by a response of love. So it is in the relationship between God and ourselves. God had no need to create the world, but once created he has allowed himself to be affected by us. He invites us to co-operate with him in the achievement of his purpose: he wants our positive response; he can be hurt as he can be made glad. Of this truth the incarnation and cross is the supreme expression and definitive revelation. This is a truth brought out well in a Christmas sermon by Lewis's friend Austin Farrer:

> Yet Mary holds her finger out, and a divine hand closes on it. The maker of the world is born a begging child; he begs for milk, and does not know that it is milk for which he begs. We will not lift our hands to pull the love of God down to us, but he lifts his hands to pull human compassion down upon his cradle. So the weakness of God proves stronger than men, and the folly of God proves wiser than men. Love is the strongest instrument of omnipotence, for accomplishing those tasks he cares most dearly to perform; and this is how he brings his love to bear on human pride; by weakness not by strength, by need and not by bounty.[4]

"The maker of the world is born a begging child." He

makes himself dependent on the love of his family. Later he comes to need the support and love of his friends. It is a mistake to think that the love between Jesus and his followers was all one-way. However much they let him down and failed him, he needed them.

There are, as we should expect, many fine insights and trenchant warnings in *The Four Loves*. Lewis gives us a more sensitive and comprehensive analysis of love than the Swedish theologian Anders Nygen, in his *Agape and Eros*, a book which set the theological mood on this subject for the three decades in which Lewis was writing popular theology. But Lewis did not quite take the full measure of an incarnational view of God; a God who puts himself in the position of needing us. We need him, of course, in all we think and do and say. But God also invites us to share with him in the achievement of his purposes. He comes amongst us to make that invitation explicit. He tells us that he needs us.

It is probably useless to speculate – nevertheless there is an irresistible temptation to do so – about whether, if Lewis had written another book about love towards the end of his life, it would have been different from *The Four Loves*. For most of his life Lewis interpreted Christian love in terms of unselfish giving. He was heroic in his correspondence to people who wrote to him from all over the world. This natural inclination of Christian love as giving was reinforced in his case by the impermeable exterior he presented to most of the world. Behind that exterior, we know, there was much pain and longing. But it was not a side that he felt able to show to others. With the coming of Joy Davidman into his life he was turned upside down. He gave to her, of course, but he also discovered that he needed her as he had needed no other human being. Then when she died there was the experience of being totally broken. It was a very much more sensitive and vulnerable Lewis who wrote *A Grief Observed* and *Prayer: Letters to Malcolm* than the one who wrote *The Four Loves*. For *The Four Loves*, despite its rejection of crude over-simplifications, despite its many insights, does not always appeal. Indeed, one of the most loving people I know told me once that he really hated the book. If Lewis had written another book on love towards the end of his life it would surely have reflected more strongly his own experience of need and brokenness. In particular this would have modified his understanding of God as all-powerful. For Lewis worked with a model, sophisticated and properly qualified, but none the less dominant, of an all-powerful God. In the light of his own experience he might have moved more explicitly to affirm a God who is humble and lowly of heart; a God who has taken the risk of creation; who has himself been broken on the rack of it, and who invites us to share in the pain and joy of transforming it.

CHAPTER NINE

Eternal Glory

When C.S. Lewis was a student at Oxford he came to know an old Irish parson, dirty, gabbling and tragic, who had long since lost his faith but retained his living. His only interest in life was the search for evidence of human survival, about which he talked non-stop. He did not seek the Beatific vision for he did not believe in God. He didn't even seek reunion with his friends. All he wanted was some assurance that something he could call himself would outlive his bodily life. Lewis said that this state of mind appeared to him as the most contemptible he had ever encountered, and the whole question of immortality became disgusting to him.[1]

The result of this experience was that when he eventually came to believe in God he did not at the same time come to believe in an after-life. For a year he believed in God without any such belief, and came to think that it was one of the greatest mercies that had been allowed him that this should have been so. For this had been the experience of the Jews of old. For many centuries they believed in God and tried to obey his commands without any solid belief in a future existence. This gave them a strong sense of acknowledging God for his own sake and doing right just because it is right. So with Lewis. The strong, moral side of him was always on hand to urge obedience to the moral law, whether or not there is a heaven.[2] It is ironic therefore that in the maturity of his faith few people in our century have had the thought of heaven and hell so much in the forefront of their minds. Perhaps the biggest change that has taken place in the churches this century is the decline in the belief of an after-life. Public opinion polls not only show that hardly fifty per cent of the country believe in it, but, what is more surprising, the percentage is not much higher even amongst regular churchgoers. It is almost as though for many Christians belief in heaven has become an optional extra for the more pious; a fringe benefit, as it were. But in C.S. Lewis's developed faith the prospect of eternity was central. As much as for his mediaeval forebears, life was a struggle to attain heaven and avoid hell, whilst at the same time cutting down to a minimum the time in purgatory. As much as for his Victorian forebears he thought the hope of heaven ought to be a real consolation for those grieving the death of loved ones. Right at the end of his life, Lewis said that even if there was no after-life he would still want to die on the right side, with God and Christ. But, if you do believe in heaven, he continued, how can it not be central? In his work *Prayer: Letters to Malcolm* he attended to the criticism that there was too much of the supernatural in his position, especially in the sense that the next world loomed so large. But, as he said:

How can it loom less than large if it is believed in at all? ...

If that other world is once admitted, how can it, except by sensual or bustling pre-occupations, be kept in the background of our minds? How can the "rest of Christianity" – what is this "rest"? – be disentangled from it?[3]

It is quite clear then that Lewis did not have a selfish interest in his own survival of death. What he did have was a passionate concern for the cause of God, and he believed that this cause only found its final goal and victory in heaven. It is the whole character of God and Christ that is at stake. For how can we believe that the one in whom Jesus trusted really is a loving father? Jesus put his whole trust in the one he called Abba, but died with the words "My God, my God, why hast thou forsaken me?" Why should we believe that this God, who apparently let him down, is a God of love? Lewis put the answer most vividly in one of his books for children. In *The Lion, the Witch and the Wardrobe* the whole earth has been frozen over by the White Witch. Aslan, the great, glorious lion, comes to rescue his children but is killed, or rather, gives his life as a voluntary sacrifice. Lucy, Susan and the other children come to the altar on which Aslan lies dead and tied down with cords. But his body is no longer there:

"Who's done it?" cried Susan. "What does it mean? Is it magic?"
    "Yes!" said a great voice behind their backs. "It is more magic." They looked round. There, shining in the sunrise, larger than they had seen him before, shaking his mane (for it had apparently grown again) stood Aslan himself.

"Oh, Aslan!" cried both the children, staring up at him, almost as much frightened as they were glad.

"Aren't you dead then, dear Aslan?" said Lucy.

"Not now," said Aslan. ...

"But what does it all mean?" asked Susan when they were somewhat calmer.

"It means," said Aslan, "that though the Witch knew the Deep Magic, there is a magic deeper still which she did not know. Her knowledge goes back only to the dawn of time. But if she could have looked a little further back, into the stillness and the darkness before Time dawned, she would have read there a different incantation. She would have known that when a willing victim who had committed no treachery was killed in a traitor's stead, the Table would crack and Death itself would start working backwards. And now –" ...

"Oh, children, I feel my strength coming back to me. Oh, children, catch me if you can!" He stood for a second, his eyes very bright, his limbs quivering, lashing himself with his tail. Then he made a leap high over their heads and landed on the other side of the Table. Laughing, though she didn't know why, Lucy scrambled over it to reach him. Aslan leaped again. A mad chase began. Round and round the hill-top he led them, now hopelessly out of their reach, now letting them almost catch his tail, now diving between them, now tossing them in the air with his huge and beautifully velveted paws and catching them again, and now stopping unexpectedly so that all three of them rolled over together in a happy laughing heap of fur and arms and legs. It was such a romp as no one has ever had except in Narnia; and whether it was more like playing with a thunderstorm or playing with a kitten Lucy could never make up her mind.[4]

Christ raised from the dead, the decisive sign of God's goodwill towards us and his promise of immortality to those who allow their lives to be raised from the death of sin with Christ. That was the foundation of Lewis's belief in heaven. Nevertheless, despite all his earlier feelings on the subject, when his wife died he claimed to have some clear assurance of her continuing reality in God. In the early part of the notebook he kept after her death, later published as *A Grief Observed*, he was his usual scornful self about spiritualist pictures of reunion with the departed. He regarded such pictures as unscriptural and contradictory of the general truth that "reality never repeats".[5] Yet, later in the notebook, he records an experience that took him by surprise and that was quite unlike anything he had imagined.

> It was quite incredibly unemotional. Just the impression of her *mind* momentarily facing my own. Mind, not "soul" as we tend to think of soul. Not at all like a rapturous reunion of lovers. Much more like getting a telephone call or a wire from her about some practical arrangement. Yet there was an extreme and cheerful intimacy. An intimacy that had not passed through the senses or the emotions at all.[6]

Lewis commented afterwards that if this was a throw-up from his unconscious, then his unconscious was a much more interesting place than he thought and much less primitive than his conscious mind. For the idea it had thrown up was the idea of pure intelligence, a Greek rather than a Hebrew idea. And whereas he had in the past dismissed such a prospect as arid and chilling, it made him wonder whether there could not after all be a communion of pure intelligences that had this utterly reliable, firm intimacy about it.

If the resurrection of Christ is the foundation of Christian belief in heaven, for Lewis it was also the tantalizing experience of joy that pointed to the possibility of an abiding joy. It was reflection on the experience of joy when he was an atheist that helped lead Lewis to faith. And when he tried to picture heaven it was in images drawn from play and relaxation, images of music and dancing. These images may seem frivolous to us but they were, thought Lewis, the only ones that could do justice to the spontaneity and liberation of heaven. There everything is different. On this earth games and dancing may seem frivolous but "Joy is the serious business of heaven".[7]

Joy and glory. It was in writing about glory that the passions of Lewis the Romantic and the Christian, the literary critic and the believer, fused together in a marvellous whole. For he believed, as indeed St Paul believed, that we really will be glorified; transfigured in our whole being:

We do not want merely to *see* beauty, though, God knows, even that is bounty enough. We want something else which can hardly be put into words – to be united with the beauty we see, to pass into it, to receive it into ourselves, to bathe in it, to become part of it. … That is why the poets tell us such lovely falsehoods. They talk as if the west wind could really sweep into a human soul; but it can't. They tell us that "beauty born of murmuring" will pass into a human face;

but it won't. Or not yet. For if we take the imagery of scripture seriously, if we believe that God will one day *give* us the Morning Star and cause us to *put on* the splendour of the sun, then we may surmise that both the ancient myths and the modern poetry, so false as history, may be very near the truth as prophecy. At present we are on the outside of the world, the wrong side of the door. We discern the freshness and purity of morning, but they do not make us fresh and pure. We cannot mingle with the splendours we see. But all the leaves of the New Testament are rustling with the rumour that it will not always be so. Some day, God willing, we shall get *in*. When human souls have become as perfect in voluntary obedience as the inanimate creation is in its lifeless obedience, then they will put on its glory, or rather that greater glory of which nature is only the first sketch.[8]

Yet how can these things be? For as the hymn puts it, "Change and decay in all around I see." "Time like an ever rolling stream bears all her sons away." Everything we have loved and valued is taken remorselessly into the ever receding past. Yet there is one way in which the past can be retained; through the power of memory. And towards the end of his life Lewis developed some interesting speculations on this theme. He did not, any more than most of us, believe the old picture of resurrection whereby the bits of our corpse come together and we then climb out of the ground. Our physical bodies become part of the earth and are taken into the cycle of nature. But, he argued, it is not matter as such that really concerns us, but our sensations. What the soul cries out for is the resurrection of the senses. Matter only counts for us because it is the source of our

sensations. And we already have some feeble and inter-
mittent power of raising dead sensations from the grave
through memory. Memory brings the past into the
present. By that Lewis did not mean that the dead will
simply have the power of remembering earthly sensations, rather, the other way round. Our memory now is
but a foretaste, a mirage even, of a power which the soul
will exercise hereafter. There will, however, be two
differences. Our power to recall the past will not come
and go but will be permanent. Secondly, memory will not
be private. I can now tell you about the vanished fields of
my childhood only imperfectly and in words. Then I will
be able to take you for a walk through them. It is a
mistake, thought Lewis, to dismiss memories as being
inferior to the original experience. If we went back to the
wheatfield we might see stalks of grain-bearing grass. It
is the transfiguring power of memory that remembers
our visit as "orient and immortal wheat", to use Tra-
herne's words. This power of memory to glorify the past
is the beginning of resurrection. Lewis had to face the
criticism that all this makes the after-life sound like a
dream world. But, as he pointed out, what is matter
anyway? Modern physics reveals it is mostly empty
space. Further, matter concerns us because it enters our
experience by becoming sensation, that is, by becoming
part of our soul. The element in the soul that it becomes
will be raised and glorified, not as a substitute for the
original, but bearing a relationship to it as the flower does
to the root or a diamond does to the coal. This may not
happen all at once. We may first have to go to Lenten

lands to be made ready but one day we will recover, in transfigured, glorified form, what time has borne away.

> Then the new earth and sky, the same yet not the same as these, will rise in us as we have risen in Christ. And once again, after who knows what aeons of the silence and the dark, the birds will sing out and the waters flow, and lights and shadows move across the hills and the faces of our friends laugh upon us with amazed recognition.
>   Guesses, of course, only guesses. If they are not true, something better will be. For we know that we shall be made like Him, for we shall see Him as He is.[9]

On Friday, 22nd November 1963, shortly before his sixty-fifth birthday, cared for by his brother Warnie and ministered to by Austin Farrer,[10] Lewis discovered the reality about which he had made such memorable guesses.

Notes

Geoffrey Bles was the original publisher of C.S. Lewis's theological works, and these books were later taken over by William Collins. In due course Collins put most of them into paperback under the name of Fontana, and they are currently published under the specialized imprint of Fount Paperbacks.

A complete list of the C.S. Lewis titles available from Fount is given on page 93.

Chapter One

1. Austin Farrer, *Saving Belief*, Hodder and Stoughton, 1964
2. Austin Farrer, *The Brink of Mystery*, SPCK, 1976
3. Brian Sibley, *Shadowlands*, Hodder and Stoughton, 1985

Chapter Two

1. C.S. Lewis, *Surprised by Joy*, Fontana, 1959, pp. 18f.
2. C.S. Lewis, *Surprised by Joy*, Fontana, 1959, p. 20.
3. C.S. Lewis, *Surprised by Joy*, Fontana, 1959, p. 119.
4. C.S. Lewis, *Surprised by Joy*, Fontana, 1959, p. 136.
5. C.S. Lewis, *Surprised by Joy*, Fontana, 1959, p. 135.
6. C.S. Lewis, *Surprised by Joy*, Fontana, 1959, p. 176.
7. C.S. Lewis, *A Grief Observed*, Faber, 1961, p. 10.
    See also *Surprised by Joy*, p. 137.
8. C.S. Lewis, *Surprised by Joy*, Fontana, 1959, p. 176.

9. e.g. by John Beversluis, *C.S. Lewis and the Search for Rational Religion*, Eerdmans, 1985.
    This book is well worth reading by those who wish to probe more critically, but still sympathetically, into Lewis's work. I have referred to his criticisms at a number of points in this book.
10. Simone Weil, *Waiting on God*, Fontana, 1959, p. 121.
11. C.S. Lewis, *Surprised by Joy*, Fontana, 1959, p. 182.
12. "The Weight of Glory" in C.S. Lewis, *Screwtape Proposes a Toast*, Fontana, 1965, pp. 97f.

Chapter Three

1. C.S. Lewis, *The Problem of Pain*, Fontana, 1957, p. 41.
2. C.S. Lewis, *A Grief Observed*, Faber, 1961, pp. 35f.
3. C.S. Lewis, *A Grief Observed*, Faber, 1961, p. 60.

Chapter Four

1. C.S. Lewis, *The Screwtape Letters*, Fount, 1977, pp. 29–32.
2. C.S. Lewis, *The Great Divorse*, Fount, 1977, pp. 37f.
3. Published in C.S. Lewis, *Screwtape Proposes a Toast*, Fontana, 1965, pp. 28–40.
4. Austin Farrer, *The Brink of Mystery*, SPCK, 1976, p. 46.
5. C.S. Lewis, *Poems*, Geoffrey Bles, 1964, p. 129.

Chapter Five

1. C.S. Lewis, *Prayer: Letters to Malcolm*, Fount, 1977, p. 43.
2. C.S. Lewis, *The Problem of Pain*, Fontana, 1957, pp. 94f.
3. C.S. Lewis, *A Grief Observed*, Faber, 1961, p. 26.
4. "The Christian Apologist" in *Light on C.S. Lewis*, ed. Jocelyn Gibb, Bles, 1965, pp. 40f.
5. Austin Farrer, *Love Almighty and Ills Unlimited*, Fontana, 1966.

6. I have expanded these arguments in Chapter 5 of my *Being a Christian*, Mowbrays, 1981.

Chapter Six

1. Evelyn Waugh, *Brideshead Revisited*, Penguin, 1951, p. 84.
2. C.S. Lewis, *Screwtape Proposes a Toast*, Fontana, 1965, p. 42.
3. C.S. Lewis, *God in the Dock*, Fount, 1979, p.7.
4. "Myth became Fact" in C.S. Lewis, *God in the Dock*, Fount, 1979, pp. 44f.
5. 2 Corinthians 8:9.
6. Philippians 2:5–8.

Chapter Seven

1. C.S. Lewis, *Surprised by Joy*, Fontana, 1959, p. 182.
2. C.S. Lewis, *Prayer: Letters to Malcolm*, Fount, 1977, p. 81.
3. C.S. Lewis, *Prayer: Letters to Malcolm*, Fount, 1977, pp. 91f.
4. "Petitionary Prayer: A Problem without an Answer", C.S. Lewis, *Christian Reflections*, Fount, 1981, pp. 180–90.
5. C.S. Lewis, *Prayer: Letters to Malcolm*, Fount, 1977, p. 63.
6. C.S. Lewis, *A Grief Observed*, Faber, 1961, pp. 26f.
7. "The Efficacy of Prayer", C.S. Lewis, *Fern-Seed and Elephants*, Fount, 1977, pp. 96–103.
8. C.S. Lewis, *Prayer: Letters to Malcolm*, Fount, 1977, pp. 46f.

Chapter Eight

1. C.S. Lewis, *The Four Loves*, Fount, 1977, pp. 82f.
2. C.S. Lewis, *The Four Loves*, Fount, 1977, p. 21.
3. C.S. Lewis, *The Four Loves*, Fount, 1977, p. 116.
4. Austin Farrer, *Said or Sung*, Faith Press, 1960.

Chapter Nine

1. C.S. Lewis, *Surprised by Joy*, Fontana, 1959, pp. 162f.
2. C.S. Lewis, *Surprised by Joy*, Fontana, 1959, pp. 184f.
3. C.S. Lewis, *Prayer: Letters to Malcolm*, Fount, 1977, p. 119f.
4. C.S. Lewis, *The Lion, The Witch and the Wardrobe*, Bles, 1950, Fontana Lions, 1980. pp. 147–9.
5. C.S. Lewis, *A Grief Observed*, Faber, 1961, p. 25.
6. C.S. Lewis, *A Grief Observed*, Faber, 1961, pp. 56f.
7. C.S. Lewis, *Prayer: Letters to Malcolm*, Fount, 1977, p. 95.
8. "The Weight of Glory" in C.S. Lewis, *Screwtape Proposes a Toast*, Fontana, 1965, pp. 106f.
9. C.S. Lewis, *Prayer: Letters to Malcolm*, Fount, 1977, p. 124.
10. After Lewis's death it was sometimes said that his mantle had fallen on Farrer. In fact no Christian writer has achieved Lewis's popularity. Farrer, who died in 1968, was a more sensitive spirit than Lewis and had an even more subtle mind. Perhaps for these reasons he has not reached Lewis's public. My anthology of Farrer's writings, *The One Genius: Through the Year with Austin Farrer*, SPCK, 1987, was compiled to try to make him more accessible.

Books by C.S. Lewis available as Fount Paperbacks

The Abolition of Man
Boxen (illustrated)
The Business of Heaven
Christian Reflections
The Dark Tower
Fern-Seed and Elephants
First and Second Things
The Four Loves
God in the Dock
The Great Divorce
Letters to Children
Mere Christianity
Miracles
Of This and Other Worlds
The Pilgrim's Regress
Prayer: Letters to Malcolm
Present Concerns
The Problem of Pain
Reflections on the Psalms
The Screwtape Letters
Screwtape Proposes a Toast
Surprised by Joy

Available as Fontana Lions
The Chronicles of Narnia
(seven volumes)

Also available in Fount Paperbacks

BOOKS BY C. S. LEWIS

Christian Reflections

'This collection . . . deserves the warmest of Christian welcomes on this happy reappearance . . . a devastating counter-attack on the "new morality" and a magnificent restatement of the essence of the Gospel and the faith.'

Church Times

The Four Loves

'He has never written better. Nearly every page scintillates with observations which are illuminating, provocative and original.'

Church Times

Prayer: Letters to Malcolm

'A book full of wisdom, of bitter honesty and of deep charity. It nowhere tells us "how to pray" but . . . stimulates afresh that hunger and thirst for God without which we should never pray at all.'

J. B. Phillips

The Pilgrim's Regress

'A welcome reappearance in paperback. Bunyanesque in form, as the title suggests, this reissue may well pick up a new generation of readers . . .'

Methodist Recorder

Also available in Fount Paperbacks

BOOKS BY C. S. LEWIS

Reflections on the Psalms

'Absolutely packed with wisdom. It is clearly the fruit of very much
reflection . . . upon one's own darkness of spirit, one's own fumbling
and grasping in the shadows of prayer or of penitence.'

Trevor Huddleston

Miracles

'This is a brilliant book, abounding in lucid exposition and
illuminating metaphor.'

Charles Davey, The Observer

The Problem of Pain

'Written with clarity and force, and out of much knowledge and
experience.'

Times Literary Supplement

Surprised by Joy

'His outstanding gift is clarity. You can take it at two levels, as
straight autobiography, or as a kind of spiritual thriller, a
detective's probing of clue and motive . . .'

Isabel Quigley, Sunday Times

Fount Paperbacks

Fount is one of the leading paperback publishers of religious books and below are some of its recent titles.

- ☐ THE WAY OF THE CROSS Richard Holloway £1.95
- ☐ LIKE WIND ON THE GRASSES Rita Snowden £1.95
- ☐ AN INTRODUCTION TO MARITAL
     PROBLEMS Jack Dominian £2.50
- ☐ I AM WITH YOU John Woolley £2.95
- ☐ NOW AND FOR EVER Anne Townsend £1.95
- ☐ THE PERFECTION OF LOVE Tony Castle £2.95
- ☐ A PROPHETIC PEOPLE Clifford Hill £2.95
- ☐ THOMAS MORE Richard Marius £7.95
- ☐ WALKING IN THE LIGHT David Winter £1.95
- ☐ HALF WAY Jim Thompson £2.50
- ☐ THE HEART OF THE BIBLE George Appleton £4.95
- ☐ I BELIEVE Trevor Huddleston £1.75
- ☐ PRESENT CONCERNS C. S. Lewis £1.95
- ☐ PSALMS OF PRAISE Frances Hogan £2.50
- ☐ MOTHER TERESA: CONTEMPLATIVE IN THE
     HEART OF THE WORLD Angelo Devananda £2.50
- ☐ IN THE HURRICANE Adrian Hastings £2.50

All Fount paperbacks are available at your bookshop or newsagent, or they can be ordered by post from Fount Paperbacks, Cash Sales Department, G.P.O. Box 29, Douglas, Isle of Man. Please send purchase price plus 22p per book, maximum postage £3. Customers outside the UK send purchase price, plus 22p per book. Cheque, postal order or money order. No currency.

NAME (Block letters) _____

ADDRESS_____

_____

_____